The Writer at Work™

By Richard Krzemien

this is our book buyer.

To Jen,
Best Wishes

Richard Krzemien

RESTLESS MINDS PRESS

Woodland Hills

ISBN-13: 978-0-9771257-3-9 (paperback)
ISBN-10: 0-9771257-3-4   (paperback)

ISBN-13: 978-0-9771257-4-6 (hardback)
ISBN-10: 0-9771257-4-2   (hardback)

Library of Congress Catalog Card Number: 2005907240

Contents

Acknowledgements

After years of struggling as a writer in Hollywood, I've learned a few things about the creative process. First, writing is tougher than Himalayan yak jerky in January. Of course, that's something any serious writer already knows. Second, beneath all the pain, frustration, hopelessness and despair, there's a lot of humor looking for a way to get out. I realized this when I typed "The End" on a play I had been rewriting for about fifteen years and my head fell onto my desk out of sheer emotional exhaustion. I think I stayed in that position for about an hour before I started to laugh. At that moment, as I wiped the blood from my forehead, I had an epiphany that opened the door to **The Writer at Work™.**

That insight would not have been possible had it not been for all those who believed in and supported me along the way. One person who immediately comes to mind is Jim Crocker, a talented writer/producer who was working some years ago on the update of **The Twilight Zone.** He took a big chance on me and my then writing partner Chip Duncan, by giving us our first paid Hollywood TV writing job, thereby allowing us to "write with the bulls."

Similarly, this book would not exist without the support of my wife Debra and my son Evan, as well as Phil Moscovitch, Jeff Reich, Chip Hiestand, Michelle Tullier, the contributing authors in Chapter Two, my loyal website visitors, the gifted illustrator and humorist Gary Larson, stand-up comics Steve Martin and George Carlin, my favorite visionary Gene Roddenberry and my alma mater, Southern Illinois University. Above all, I would like to thank Bruce Joel Rubin, whose unwavering encouragement helped me to "dig deeper" than I ever thought humanly possible.

Exploring the depths of writing with comics has taken me on a journey through a rich emotional landscape I'd previously overlooked. Along the way I've had a chance to take stock of those whose wit and wisdom have influenced my life. To all of them I say thank you. I hope this book, in some infinitesimal way, returns the favor.

— Richard Krzemien

P.S.   Note to aspiring writers: Listen carefully. Everything your family says will end up in your work.

Foreword

There is nothing funny about writing.

Just ask any screenwriter. It's long, lonely, and often-tedious work punctuated by bouts of self-doubt, despair, and sometimes total creative blockage. And it gets worse. If one actually manages to finish a script, and in the unlikely event that it's good, and even more unlikely event that it gets sold, chances are that it will be re-written by someone you've never met, making ten times more money for a week's work than you will possibly make in your lifetime. Most likely it will be totally reimagined and reconceptualized, and no longer have your name on it. And what's worse, many screenwriters would give their firstborn and sell their mothers for an opportunity like this.

There is nothing funny about writing.

A typical day of writing begins with answering e-mail, making dentist appointments, paying bills, cleaning your office, clipping your toenails, Windexing your computer screen, taking out the garbage and re-writing your will. Then it's time for lunch. After a nap you face the blank screen or blank page and, after a series of very personal prayers and incantations, begin to write. Three hours later you have produced the two best scenes ever written for the American screen. In celebration you take a break, eat whatever it is you reward yourself with, and then return to re-read what you have written. Amazingly, your words have suddenly gone from the pinnacle of American literature to sounding like a Taco Bell commercial and you have no idea how that happened. After contemplating hara-kiri and rescheduling your therapist, you decide to break for the day. The next morning it begins again and it never changes.

There is nothing funny about writing.

Finishing a screenplay is cause for celebration. Some of us even type "THE END" prematurely just to trick ourselves into thinking we've finished. Of course one never really ends. There's always another change, another speech, another scene to be polished. Or, if you're lucky enough to be working for a studio, there's the next draft. Studio execs never tire of suggesting a few changes, like throwing out everything after page one, or sometimes even page one. But that at least means you're employed, which means that not only do you suffer all the normal complaints of screenwriters, you get to add the pressure of deadlines and weekly calls from producers saying, "You're not done YET?!" That's when you add migraines and high blood pressure to the mix.

Which brings me to Richard Krzemien. I met this man 20-some-years ago at a Writer's Guild Conference up at Lake Arrowhead. It may say something about me, or maybe about Richard, but it took years of friendship before I realized how funny he was. Who knew that underneath that aura of writerly gloom lurked a man of transcendent powers, a comedian able to transform this existential creative struggle into something actually laugh-out-loud funny.

I began to see Richard's cartoons before I attributed them to him. My son Joshua had one tacked to his door that always made me laugh. It wasn't until Richard gave me one, framed as a gift, that I realized he had drawn it. Then I got myself on his e-mail list and started to receive one every week. I actually looked forward to them. Usually they would arrive on Monday morning and in some strange way they would tap into the gestalt of the coming week. And, to my amazement, they were always funny. How, I wondered, could any human being unearth so much humor from something so deeply and consistently unpleasant as writing?

Gradually, I began to notice that the accumulation of Richard's weekly comics was displaying a truly distinctive voice and a uniquely satisfying visual style. These comics were not only funny, they were tapping into something much deeper inside me. They were addressing what it meant to be a writer, to struggle with one's hopes and fears and doubts and ambitions. They were exploring the collective writer's consciousness and turning this very solitary profession into a shared experience. And, what's more, at the very core of this deeply personal and yet collective struggle, he found humor. Maybe I was wrong. Maybe there is something funny about writing. Who would have guessed?

— Bruce Joel Rubin
Screenwriter
Ghost (Academy Award® Best Original Screenplay), *Jacob's Ladder, My Life, Deep Impact, Stuart Little 2,* and many more that haven't gotten made ...

Chapter 1

Comics

SURVIVAL TIP #3

As a financial cushion, create alternate sources of income.

… and so the time has arrived to boldly travel the universe without movement, to raise your voices in silence and to bleed from your heads without cuts. For we are writers, we are strong and we take everything sitting down.

The perfect graduation gift.

Pressing tasks to be completed before beginning a new project.

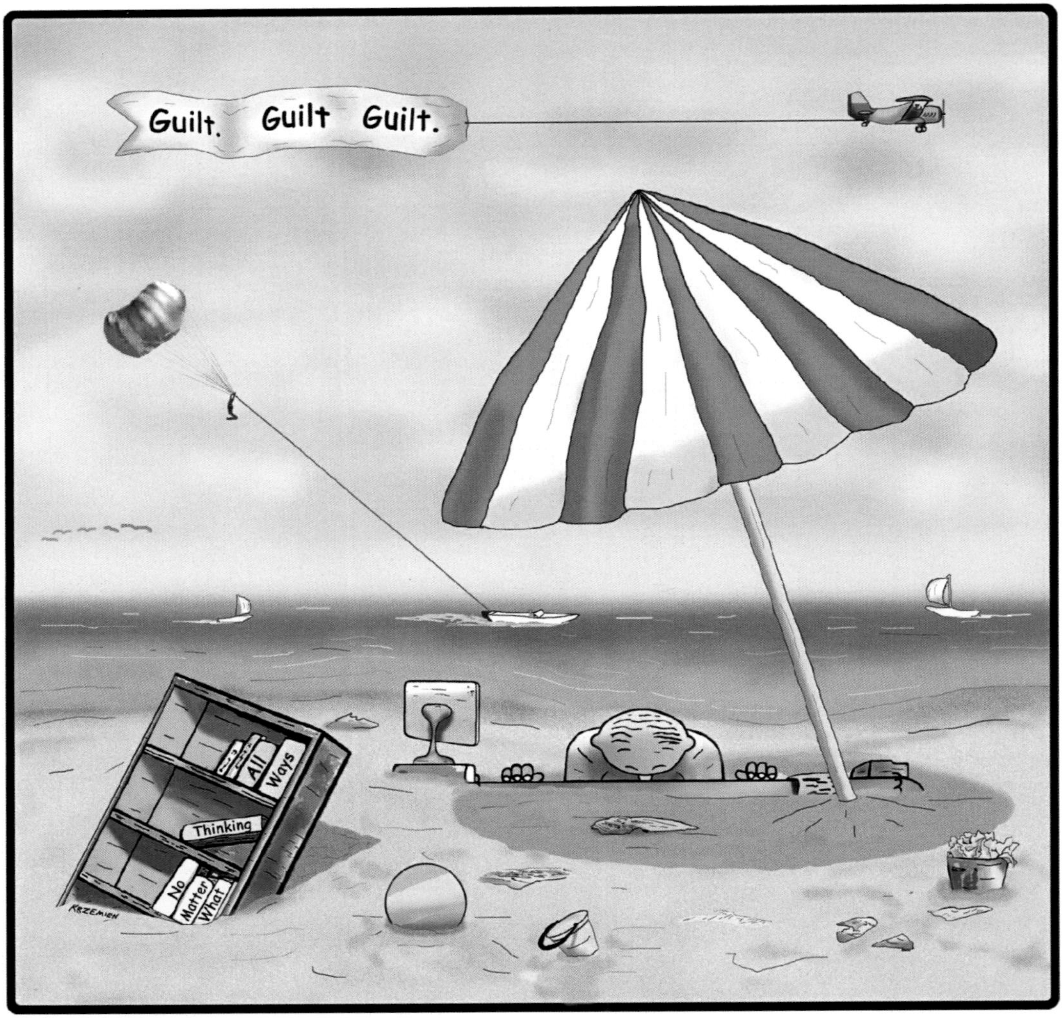
Guilt. Guilt Guilt.
All
Ways
Thinking
No
Matter
What
KRZEMIEN

The Writer at play.

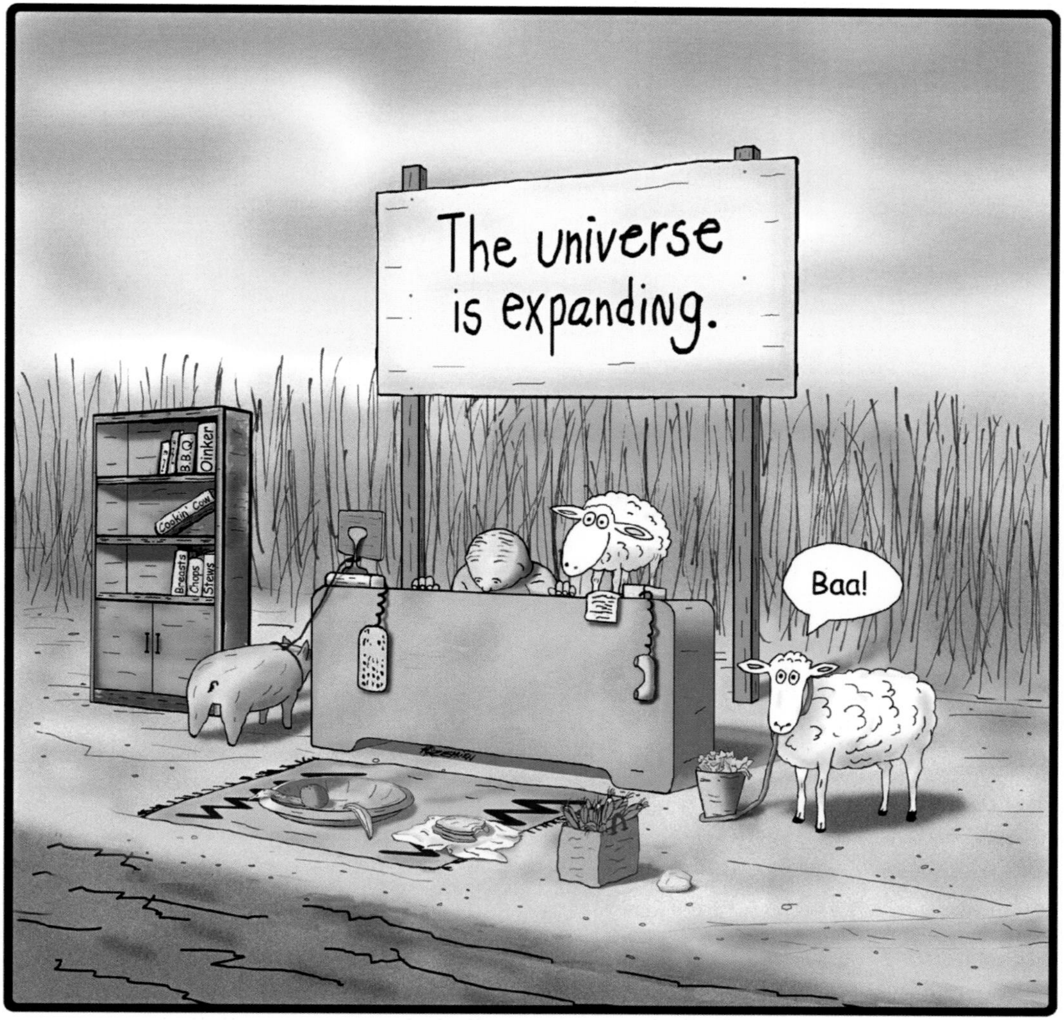
The universe is expanding.
B.B.Q
Oinker
Cookin' Cow
Breasts
Chops
Stews
Baa!

Food for thought.

Of all the burger joints in all the world…

When restaurant menu writers get writer's block.

Contents under pressure.

Alternate methods of self-promotion.

The Writer joins a mentoring program.

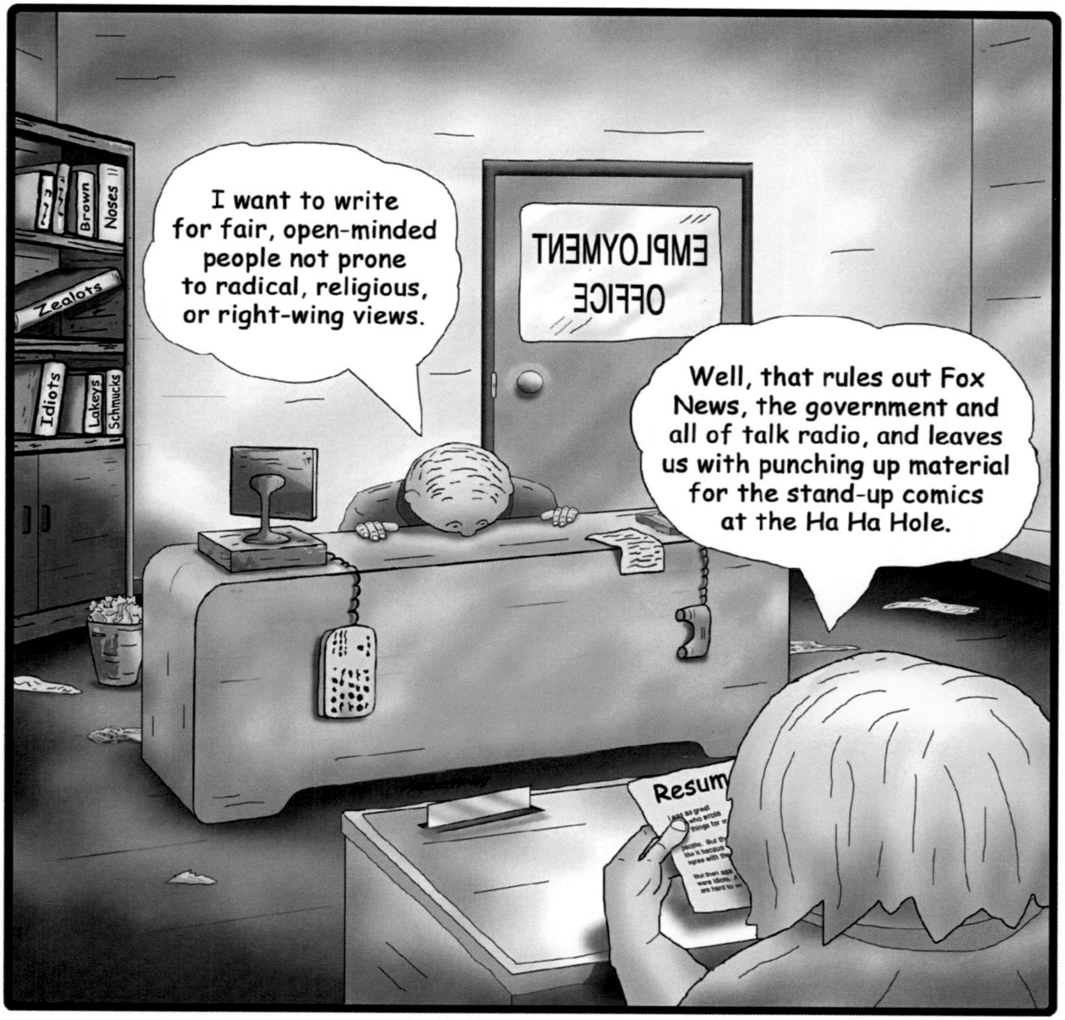
Brown
Noses
Zealots
Idiots
Lakeys
Schmucks
EMPLOYMENT
OFFICE
I want to write for fair, open-minded people not prone to radical, religious, or right-wing views.
Well, that rules out Fox News, the government and all of talk radio, and leaves us with punching up material for the stand-up comics at the Ha Ha Hole.
Resum

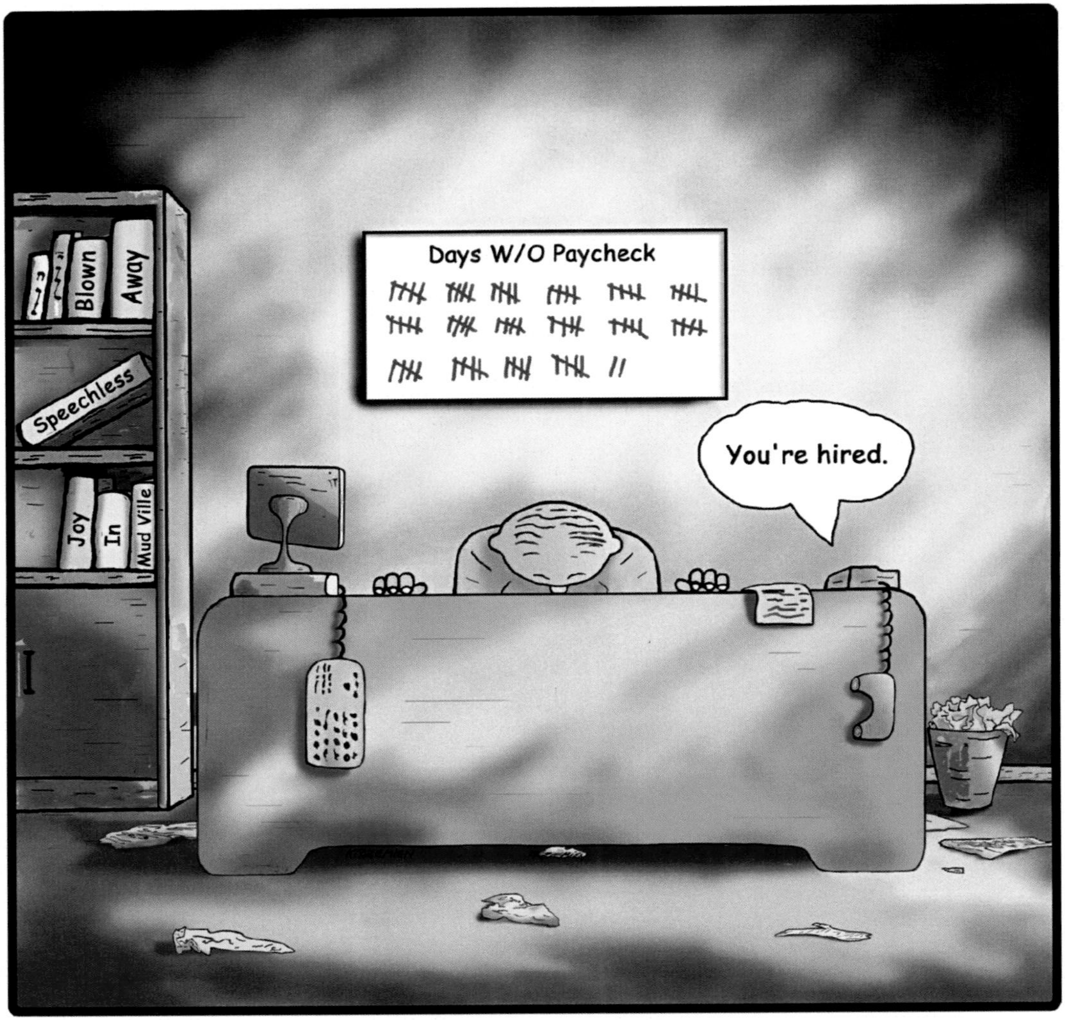
Days W/O Paycheck
Blown
Away
Speechless
Joy
In
Mud Ville
You're hired.

Shock and awe.

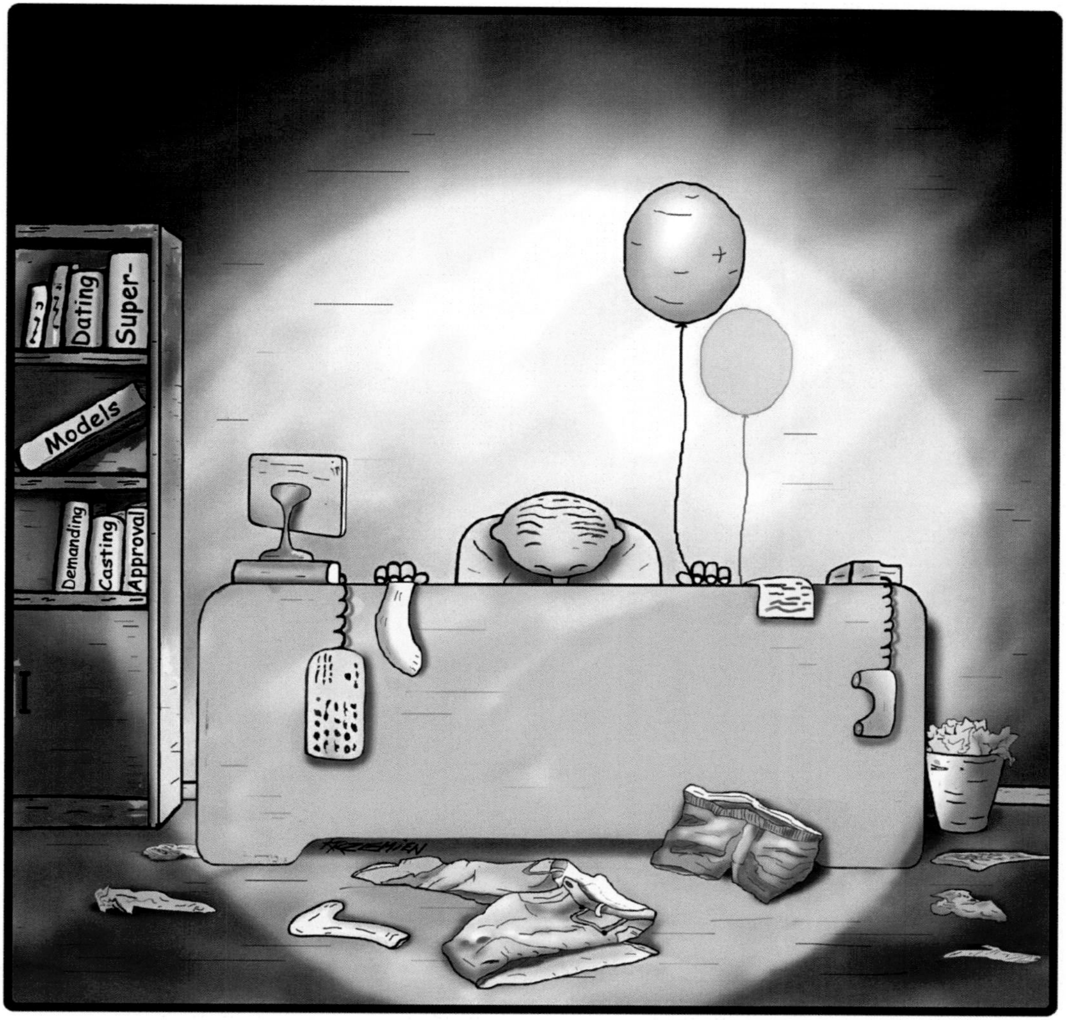
Dating
Super-
Models
Demanding
Casting
Approval

Writers gone wild.

In the early morning hours before the main event, there occurred
the fulfillment of a life-long dream: to write with the bulls.

The Writer takes a staff job.

Write the truth, even when it hurts.

Thumbs & Pencils, Inc.
Pencil Sharpener
Copier
Official
Rejection Notice

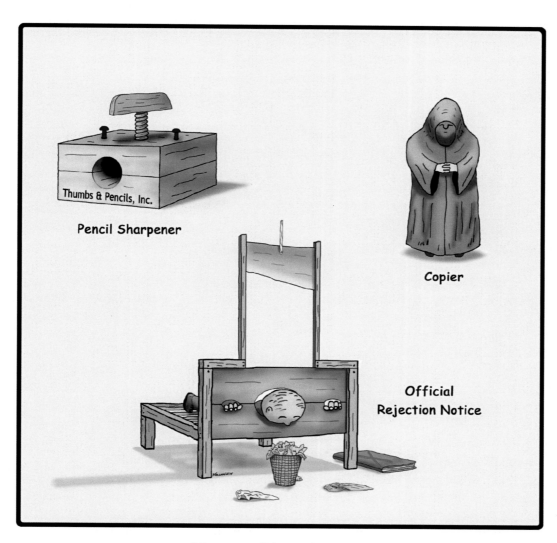

The more things change…

After years of working in a traditional manner, The Writer joins
a wilderness writers' group with mixed results.

Attending the annual Burning Writer Festival.

Advice
From
The Writer

Dear The Writer:

Q: Are there any reasons to avoid self awareness?
A: Yes. Living in the present requires more office space than
   living in the past or the future.

Q: I want my 15 minutes of fame now! I need the money.
   What do I do?
A: You're feeling panic as your biological clock awaits the birth
   of a great idea. Relax, and while you're waiting, sell a kidney.

Q: If Mad Cow disease comes from bad beef, where does
   Mad Writer disease come from?
A: Bad editors, producers, and directors.

Q: Is our inner life reflected in our outer world?
A: Well, just look around your office and you tell me.

Q: I'm feeling very small, insignificant, disposable, invisible,
   useless, unimaginative, tired, disliked by my family,
   unattractive, and that I'm a bad writer. What do I do?
A: Sounds like a typical Monday. Wait till Tuesday.
   It just gets worse.

Cynicism Lobe
Moral Outrage Lobe
B.S.
Detection
Lobe
Terror Lobe
Potty Humor
Lobe
Unbridled Joy
Sublobe

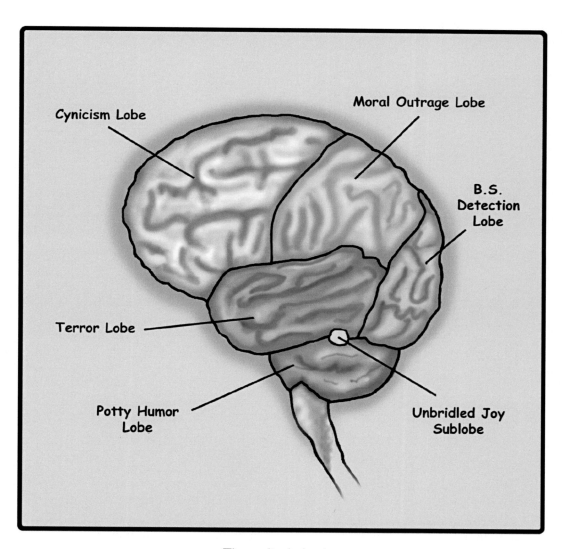

The writer's brain.

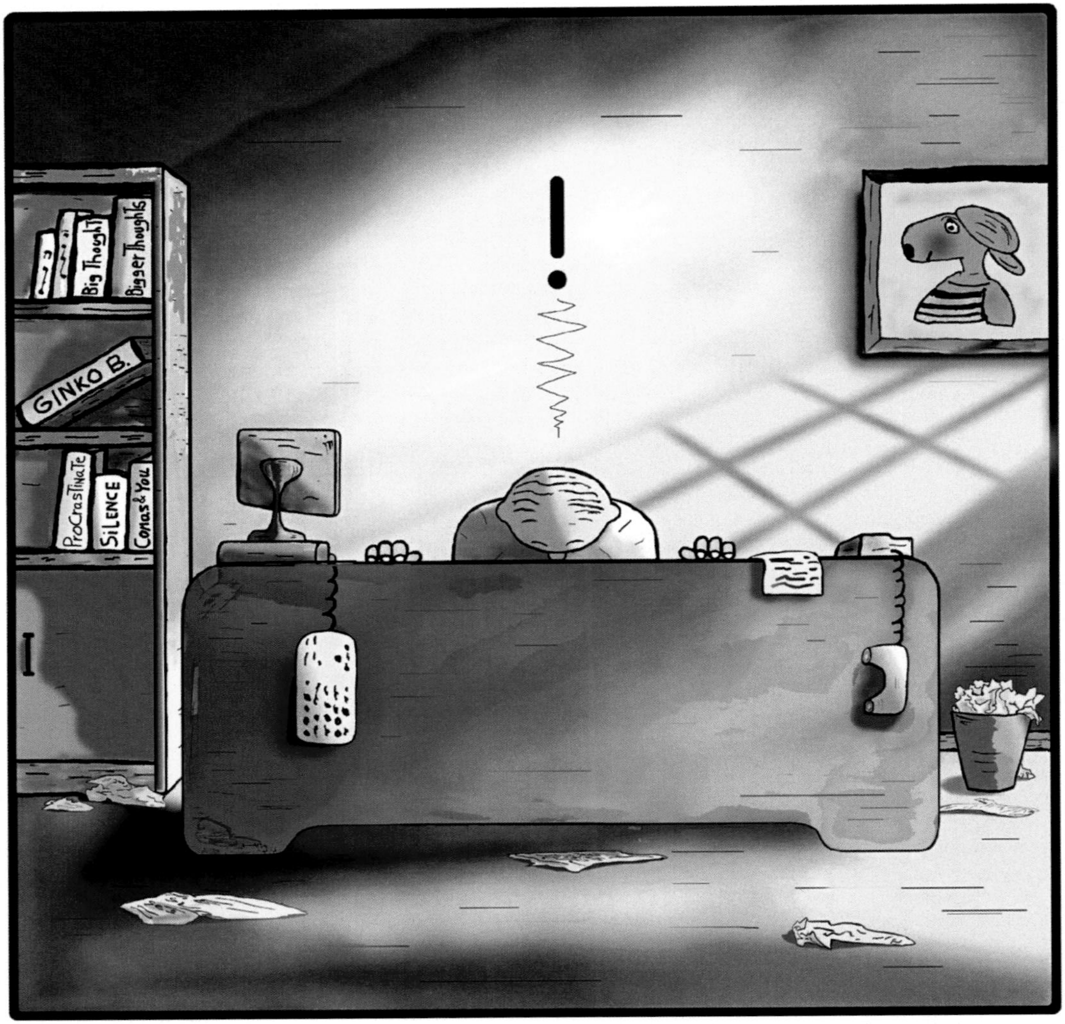
Big Thought
Bigger Thoughts
GINKO B.
ProCrastinate
SiLENCE
Conas&You
!

The unexpected arrival of inspiration sends The Writer into a creative stupor.

WRITING TIP #1

Write what you know.

Einstein's Lost Theory of Creativity:
The greater the creative effort, the stronger your desk's gravitational pull.

CAUTION:
Alternate reality under construction.

Subconscious mistakes spell checkers never catch
but significant others always do.

The Writer deliberates between two difficult choices.

After finding no willing readers for his latest revision, The Writer
is forced to solicit opinions from the creatures of the night.

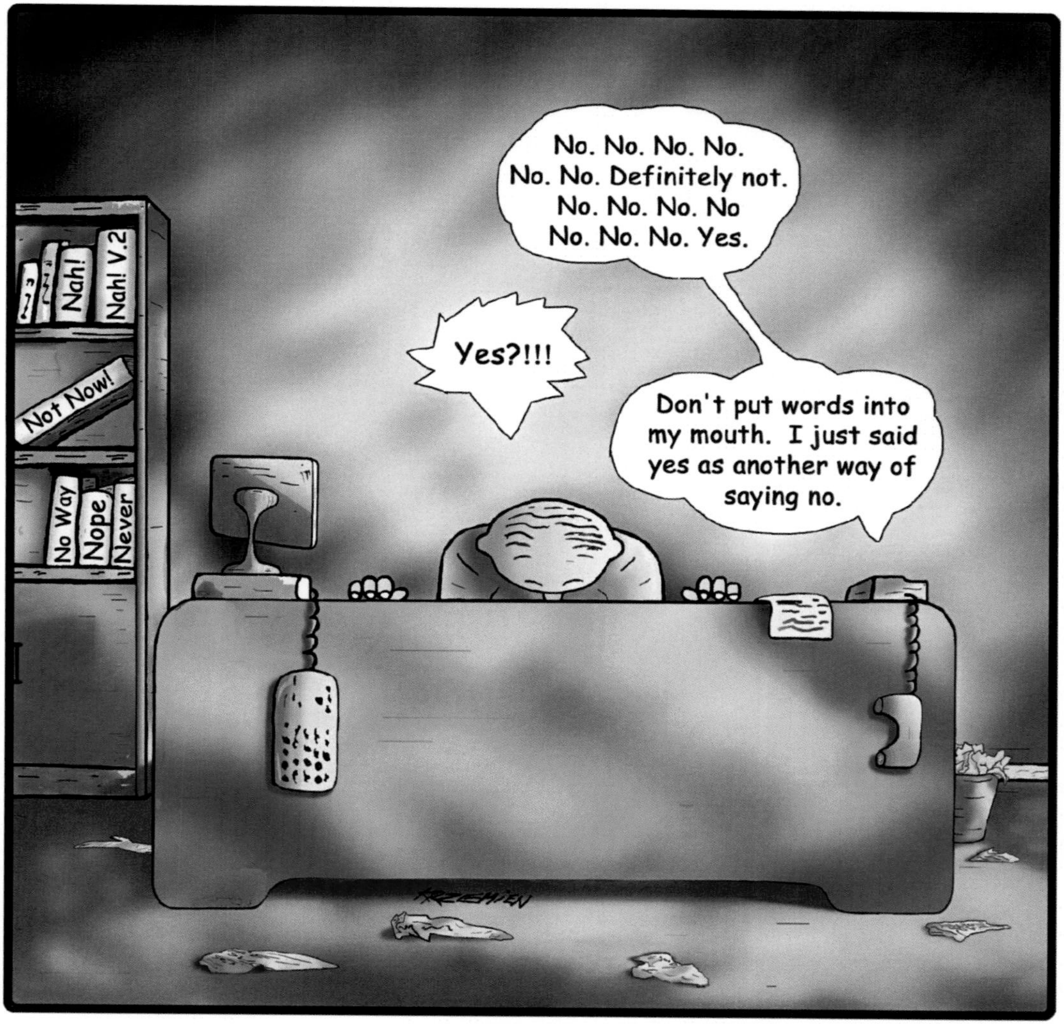
Nah!
Nah! V.2
Not Now!
No Way
Nope
Never
No. No. No. No.
No. No. Definitely not.
No. No. No. No
No. No. No. Yes.
Yes?!!!
Don't put words into my mouth. I just said yes as another way of saying no.

No.

After rolling a three, The Writer is momentarily elated.

SURVIVAL TIP #11

When feeling defeated, try using professionals like Literary Fluffers for support.

Sometimes your best ideas come late at night.

Dig deep to find your best work.

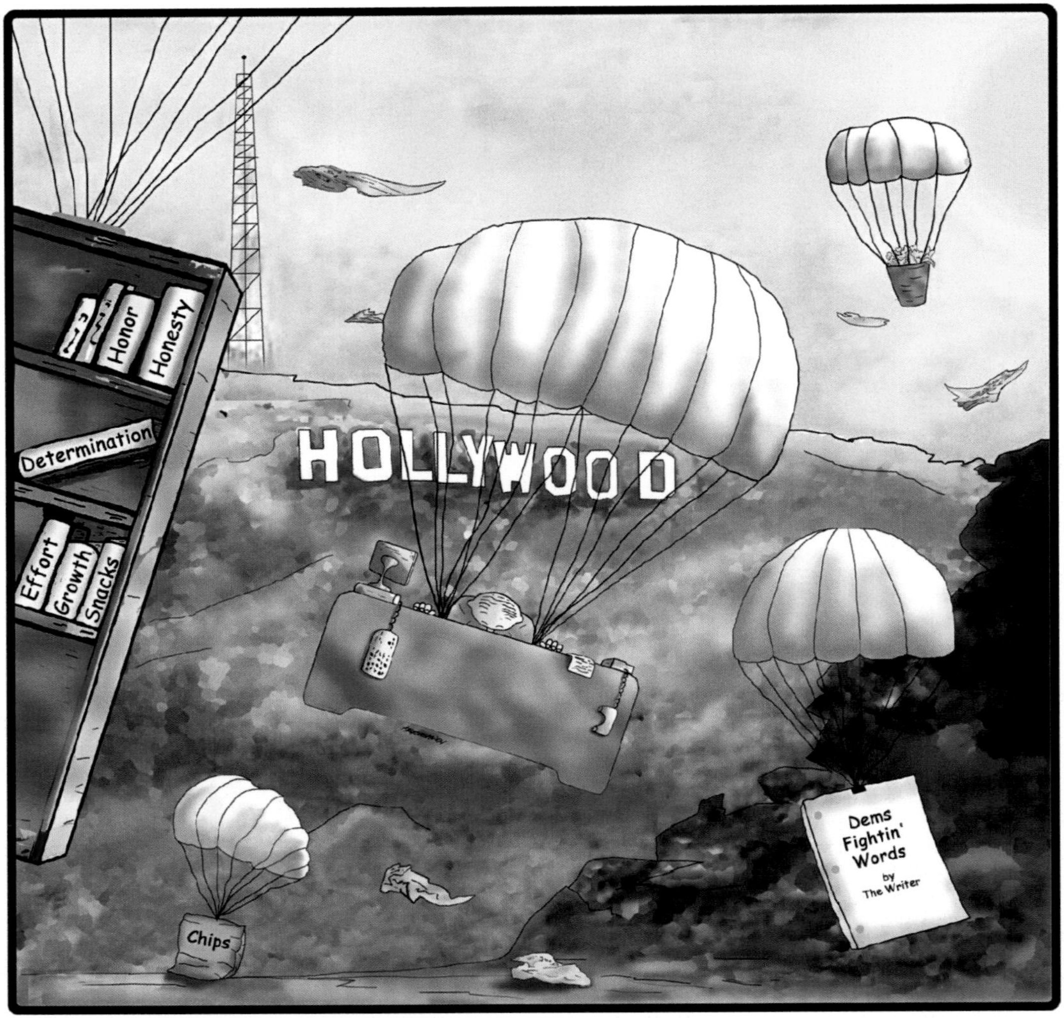
Honor
Honesty
Determination
Effort
Growth
Snacks
HOLLYWOOD
Chips
Dems
Fightin'
Words
by
The Writer

An army of one.

Existential Writing Question #2:

If the perfect Hollywood idea fell in a jungle filled with good writers,
would anyone notice?

SURVIVAL TIP #7

Always pocket a small bag of meat so sniffer dogs
find you first after a natural disaster.

The pitfalls of writing one-dimensional characters.

Protect your creative spirit.

Flu Season

Writing Season

Be prepared.

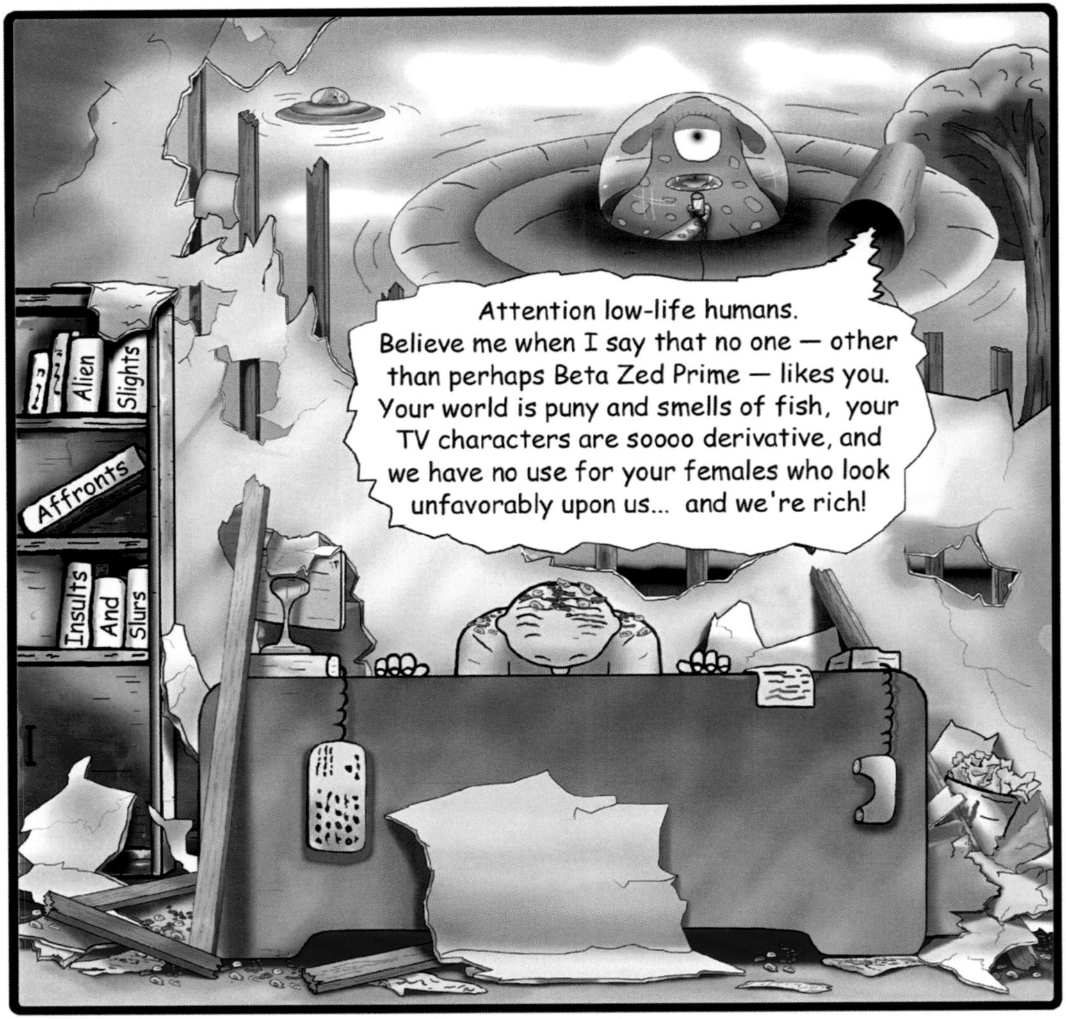
Alien
Slights
Affronts
Insults
And
Slurs
Attention low-life humans.
Believe me when I say that no one — other than perhaps Beta Zed Prime — likes you. Your world is puny and smells of fish, your TV characters are soooo derivative, and we have no use for your females who look unfavorably upon us... and we're rich!

War of the words.

While using his powers of dramatic invention, The Writer
gets caught in a tangled web of intrigue.

The reason so little is known about Schrödinger's later experiments.

Script finished, client elated, check received, all before starting the first draft.
The advantages of working in the Science Fiction genre.

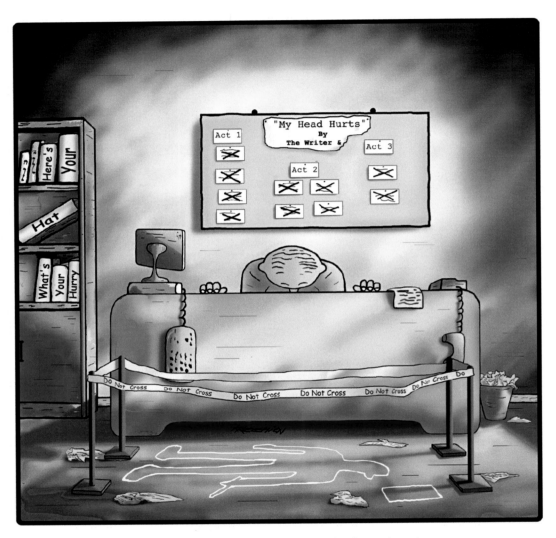

Sadly, some partnerships just don't work out.

THE AFTERLIFE
What a writer's heaven and hell might be like.

No matter how often The Writer reaches this point in the creative process, he's always startled when a large hand suddenly appears in the room.

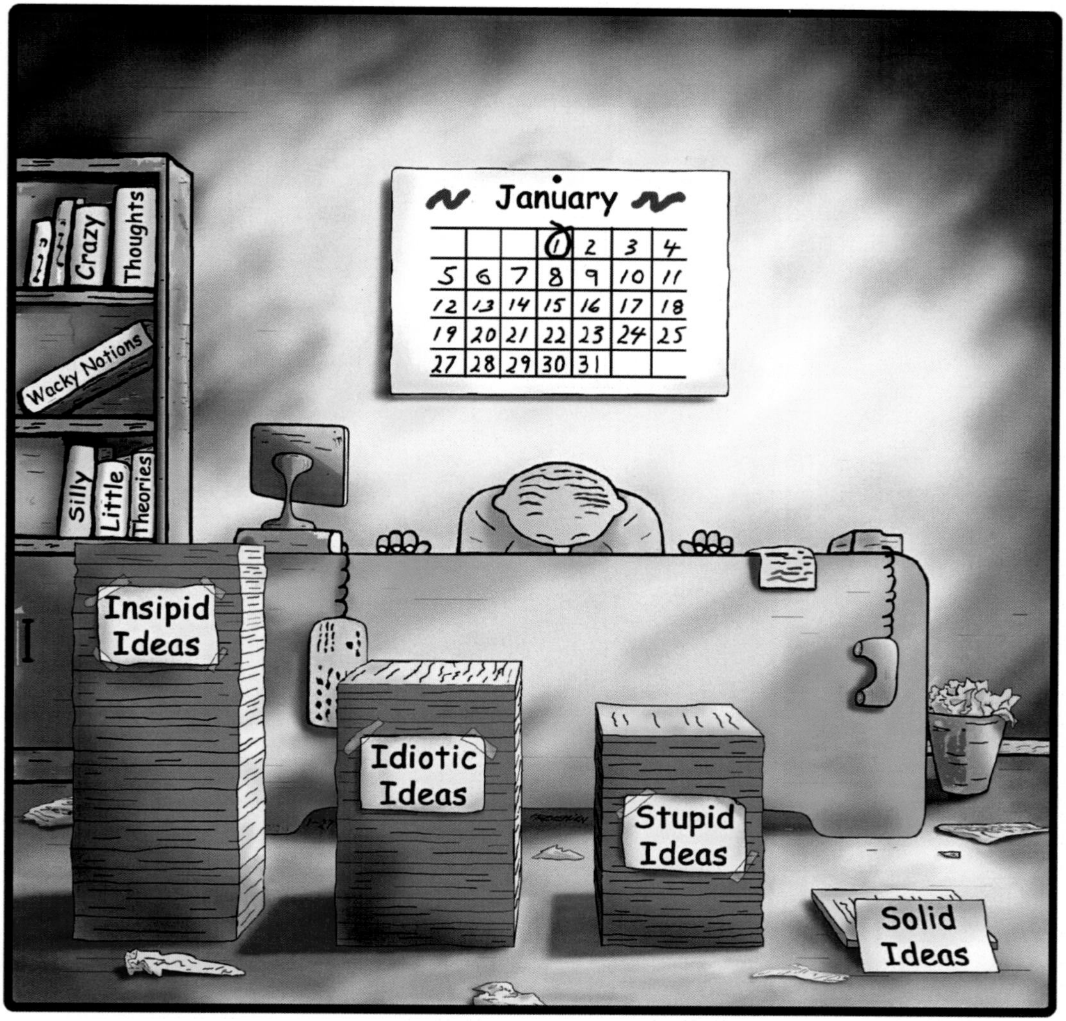
Thoughts
Crazy
Wacky Notions
Silly
Little
Theories
January
Insipid Ideas
Idiotic Ideas
Stupid Ideas
Solid Ideas

Spring cleaning.

Effort over time equals success.

Horoscope
by
The Writer

Avoid hissy fits. You hate to write but love to have written. Be near food. Suppress insanity by doing laundry. Remember, God is not on your side. Replace batteries in Big Mouth Billy Bass. Take care of minor digestive problem. Your desire to phone someone is overwhelming; resist; they're idiots! Finish something; anything. Declare a jihad on spammers. Everything your family says will end up in your work. Floss. Be open to criticism, but know you're smarter than they are. If the social elite call, speak only with Floyd.

365-Day-A-Year astrological forecast.

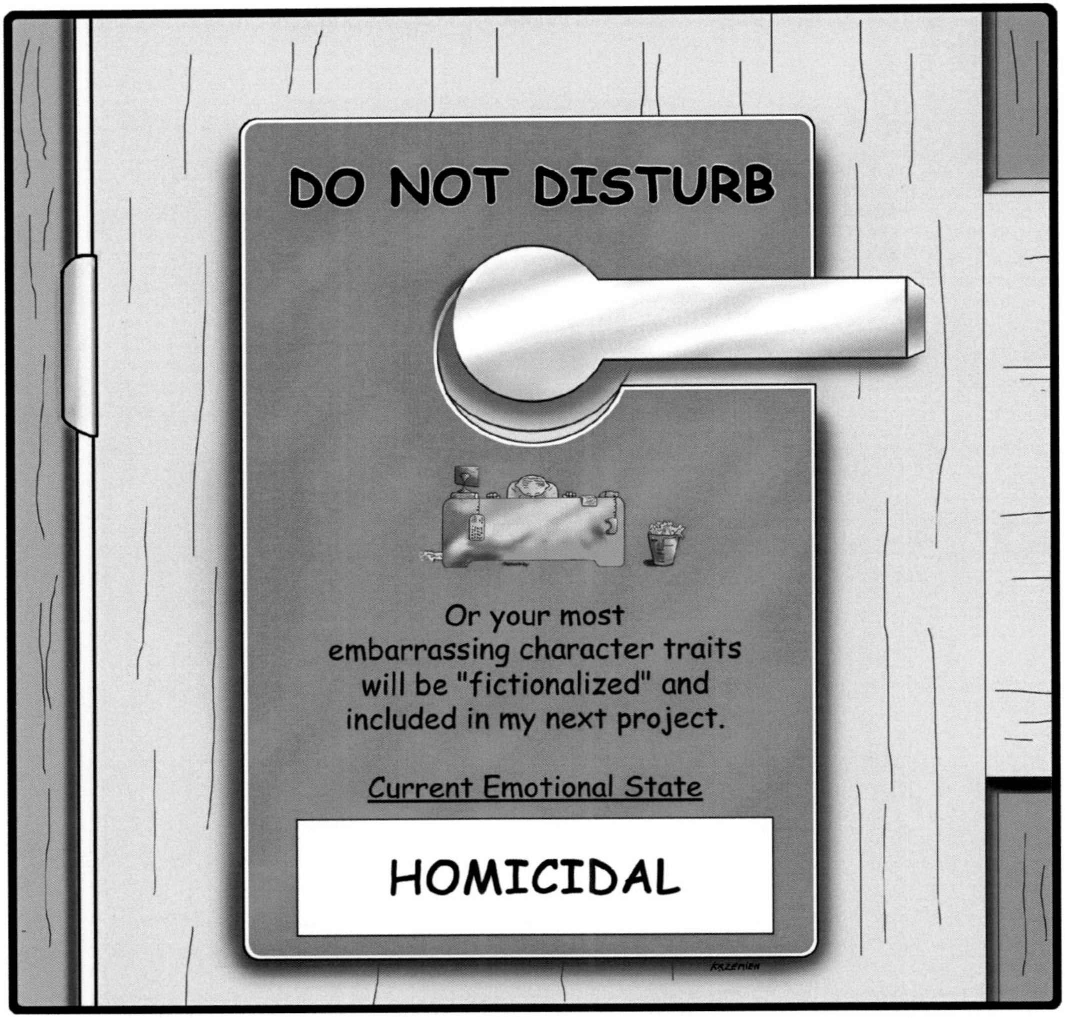
DO NOT DISTURB
Or your most
embarrassing character traits
will be "fictionalized" and
included in my next project.
Current Emotional State
HOMICIDAL
KRZEMIEN

Attending an angry bobble-headed writers' protest explains much
about why France is so hard to understand.

Always use extreme caution when handling weapons of mass instruction.

While deeply embedded in the creative process, The Writer discovers
why it takes courage to harbor an unpopular position.

Protect yourself from hostile attacks.

SURVIVAL TIP #2

Strive for balance.

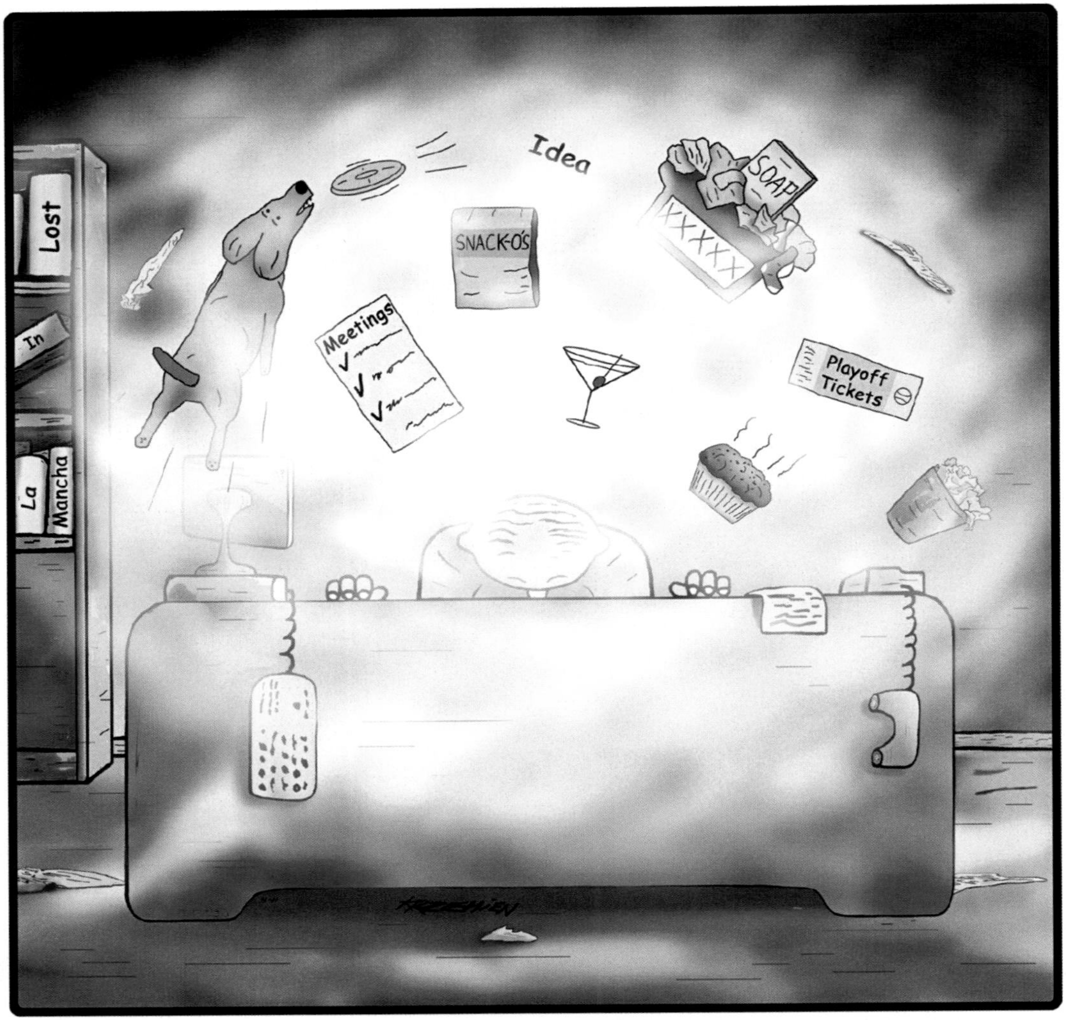
Idea
SNACK-O'S
SOAP
XXXXX
Meetings
Playoff Tickets
Lost
In
La Mancha

The fog of creativity.

Out reassessing what's important.

Give yourself the gift of peace.

From all of us to all of you...

Chapter 2

On *The Writer at Work*:

Thoughts from Working Writers
Inspired by *The Writer at Work* Comics

On Digging Deep

When writers speak of "digging deep" the implication is of a grueling undertaking to discover insightful gems. But for me the excavation is less about treasure hunting — and more about grave robbing. I am a ghoul for my buried muses.

Go back just ten generations and we have a thousand ancestors. Imagine the myriad personalities buried deep in our subconscious: fools and philosophers, saints and sinners, wise men and con men — they're all within us. Writers know when we have dug deep enough to release these subliminal beings. They appear on the scene fully formed and what they have to say seems so much more insightful and witty and passionate and honest and original than anything we could come up with. We become mere transcribers — and willingly so.

I prefer to write longhand, the pen serving as a kind of planchette that channels what my characters have to say. The word processor seems too cold and logical and organized for them. It spooks them and they remain strangely mute. Every writer, I imagine, must learn the quirks of his or her own buried spirits — what it takes to coax them up from the depths. It's worth the effort. They're such good company.

— Kevin McCarey
EMMY & Peabody Award-Winning Writer / Director
e-mail: kmccarey@hotmail.com

On Self-Esteem

On especially lovely days you might receive an e-mail or letter (if you get a phone call for a rejection, take it as a compliment) that goes into detail about how bad you suck. Your life will be torn apart, your innards exposed and you'll feel as though you were stuck in one of those dreams where you're running through Wal-Mart naked. But rejections such as these shouldn't cause too much ego damage. Why?

Hollywood hotshots CAN be wrong. If the first person that sees your work rips you apart, role with the punch and try someone else. The next person may love it.

In 2002, I sent a project out and the first person who received it sent back a scathing, page and a half rejection. I read with glazed eyes, words like, "embarrassment, superficial and flawed." Ouch! It still makes me feel like crap when I read it. A week later, I sold the project after a bidding war. Bazing!

— Jeremy Robinson
Best-Selling Author / Screenwriter
www.offcameraproductions.com

On Words & Pictures

While working as a copywriter for a large agency (one with a corral of critters: including a toothless tiger, a talking tuna and the tall in-the-saddle cowboy), I was called upon to work with a young art director.

She was a design head — someone who moved images and text around, never considering for a moment that words might mean something and weren't just props for her beautiful pictures.

Now here she was in my office, proud and confident with her mattress ad. But there was one small problem. The layout was all pictures, no words, not even a subhead in sight. So I asked, "What about the headline?" "Simple," she said, "Just write one — something like blank, blank, blank, with a twist."

I paused for a moment, then looked up and said, "Hey, you're right. Words, who needs 'em." We ran the ad without any copy.

Today she's a vice president and I've moved on.

— Lee Earle
Former Copywriter for a Top-5 National Ad Agency
Now Assistant Professor

On Writing What You Know

A few years ago I wrote and produced a PBS biography on the great writer, C.S. Lewis. While interviewing his former assistant, Walter Hooper, he said "Lewis didn't write anything good until he was in his early thirties because he didn't have anything to say." I certainly know what that's like, I thought.

Hooper went on to say that once Lewis had an epiphany and became a Christian, he then had something to say because he finally knew something. Before that, he was just a very good technician. Sure enough, Hooper was right. After a shaky start in the non-academic world, Lewis went on to write more than 33 books, all of which are still in print. Most reflect some element of his Christian message because that's what he felt he knew something about.

Well, I haven't had the same kind of epiphany; however, I have found that my best work in some way reflects my own experience. So on most days, when I find myself agonizing over what to write, I opt, instead, to go have an experience. Work, play, love, travel, adventure, you name it. Somehow, whatever happens, it enriches me and gives me some insight into the human condition. On a good day, I figure out a way to share it. Failing that, I do what many writers do — I read Walt Whitman and drink too much.

— Chip Duncan
EMMY Award-Winning Writer / Documentary Filmmaker
www.DuncanEntertainment.com

On Rejection

I could barely read the poorly mimeographed postcard: "Thank you for your submission, however… cannot… at this time…" My eyes felt prickly. I couldn't let that happen.

I dropped the card on the coffee table, jumped up, grabbed the rug and dragged it to the terrace. I threw the rug onto the wall, beat it and beat it and beat it. I returned inside, found the dining room rug, did the same to it, then the bedroom rugs. I tore down the curtains, threw them into the washer. The agitator whacked them back and forth. Then I squeezed and twisted them through the ringer. Then I scrubbed the bedspreads, sheets, slipcovers, tablecloth, potholders, and the tea cozy. I polished the furniture. I dragged the furniture to mid-room and scrubbed the walls, the floors, the doors, and the windows. Three days later, I had nothing left to beat or scrub. I sat down.

My every muscle ached. I looked around. The house was pristine and exuded tranquility, serenity. I picked up the postcard, went to my desk, made a REJECTION folder, inserted the postcard, and filed the folder in the cabinet. Then I picked up my pen and notebook, sat down, and began to write.

— Joyce Niles
Writer / Novelist / Teacher
www.joyceniles.com

On Lessons Learned

A number of years ago I was asked to come up with an idea for Sydney Poitier. My imagination stumbled upon what I thought was a terrific and singular concept: a contemporary version of OLIVER TWIST, with Mr. Poitier playing the modern-day equivalent of Fagin. Brashly confident, I pitched my concept to the executives at the studio Sydney then called home. When I finished, there was a long moment of silence. Then the chief exec looked me in the eye and said, "Two other writers came in and pitched that exact same take on OLIVER TWIST for Sydney a couple of days ago."

WHAT?! I was stunned. This had never happened to me before! I asked who the writers were. I wanted the names of the villains who dared to preempt me like this. Could it be they actually STOLE my idea out from under me? In the days that followed I researched these two writers within an inch of their lives. I was determined to map the route of their thievery and confront them with their dastardly deed.

Alas, in the wake of no evidence of theft being uncovered (or even hinted at), my feverish suspicion subsided and I was left with one of the uncomfortable truths about the business: ideas are in the ether. Time and again we are struck with what we feel are unique, even brilliant, creative ideas, only to discover someone else has been just as unique, just as brilliant… and beaten us to the punch!

— James Crocker
Writer / Producer
The New Twilight Zone, Deep Space Nine,
The Outer Limits, Stargate SG-1...

On The Afterlife

In the aftermath of a job layoff, I began writing as regularly as I could, disregarding the entrenched voices warning me to "get real, find another lawyer job and stop this silly writing crap." The early weeks of the novel were by far the most difficult. After I was laid off, my self-esteem had taken a real beating. Each time I sat at the computer it was an act of faith. But sit I did, and pages kept getting filled.

As I surrendered to the story, an epiphany occurred. Characters began to speak and act, and I began to hear another voice, rarely more than a whisper, taking delight in a surprising plot twist, or empathizing with a character's anguish. This whispered voice kept me coming back to the computer through the first draft.

Writing is my afterlife and my affirmation. I feel resurrected, like a man courting his true love, years after a bitter break up. Each time I write, I trust myself a little bit more, and I'm learning to appreciate the journey of the writing experience.

— Todd Whiteley
Novelist / Lawyer
Morgan Creek Prods., Fox Family Channel

About The Author

Richard Krzemien was born in Nottingham, England. He arrived on the shores of the U.S., at the tender young age of four. His formative years were spent burning anything he could get his hands on (while breaking no laws, of course) in Northlake, Illinois, a western suburb of Chicago. After attending Northern Illinois University where he studied business and music, he transferred to Southern Illinois University and earned a B.A. in Cinema & Photography. He then worked as a film intern for the University of Wisconsin—Madison, before co-founding Ulysses Films, a TV production company. Hollywood eventually beckoned and he moved to Los Angeles. Some of his TV writing credits include staff writer on **Quiz Kids Challenge,** scripts for the remake of **The Twilight Zone, War of the Worlds,** and creator of the first story to feature the infamous Ferengi in **Star Trek: The Next Generation.** He is a member of the Writers Guild of America, west. He currently lives in Woodland Hills, a suburb of Los Angeles, where he works as a writer, interactive game designer, script consultant, cartoonist and dog walker. He can be contacted by going to his website at: **www.TheWriterAtWork.com.** How he became a comic artist is a complete mystery, even to him.

Order Form

TO ORDER *The Writer at Work*™ COMIC ART BOOK VIA

Internet: Click on the Book Order Link at: www.TheWriterAtWork.com
Visa, MasterCard, Discover & AMEX accepted

Fax: Fax this completed form to: 801.681.9927

Mail: Restless Minds Press. 5624 Oso Ave., Suite 101,
Woodland Hills, CA 91367

Telephone: Call 818.430.1331. 9 am - 6 pm Pacific Time. Have your card ready.

Ship To: (Shipping address must be the same as Credit Card billing address.)

Name: _____

Address: _____

City: _____ State: _____ Zip: _____

Country: _____ Telephone: _____

E-Mail Address: _____

SALES TAX: California Residents add 8.25%

SHIPPING: All orders must be prepaid.
DOMESTIC GROUND - One Item Add: $3.95.
Each Additional Item Add $2.00. For 3-Day
Express Add $12.00 Per Order. **OVERSEAS** -
Surface: $15 Each Item. Airmail: $30.00 Each Item.

$15.95**US** x _____ = _____

CA Tax (8.25%): _____

Shipping: _____

Total Enclosed: _____

Payment: ☐ Check ☐ Credit Card
(Make check payable to Restless Minds Press.)

☐ Visa ☐ MasterCard ☐ Discover ☐ AMEX

Credit Card Number: _____

Expiration Date: Month: _____ Year: _____

Cardholder's Name: _____

Cardholder's Signature: _____

TO ORDER *The Writer at Work*™ T-SHIRTS, POSTERS, CAPS, as well as other
fun items, go online to www.TheWriterAtWork.com and click on the Store Link.